I0168277

The

Crossroads

of

HeArtache

& Healing

Sonya Fitch

Wider Perspectives Publishing   ¤ 2025 ¤   Hampton Roads, Va.

The poems and other writings in this book are the creations and property of Sonya Fitch, the author is responsible for them as such. Wider Perspectives Publishing reserves 1st run rights to this material in this form, all rights revert to author upon delivery. Author reserves all rights thereafter: Do not reproduce without permission except Fair Use practices for approved promotion or educational purposes. Author may redistribute, whole or in part, at will, for example submission to anthologies or contests.

© 2025, Sonya Richardson, including writing as Sonya Fitch
1st run complete in August 2025 Wider Perspectives Publishing, Hampton Roads, Va.

ISBN 978-1-964531-30-4

Contents

HeArtache

The Crossroads

Healing

4

Sonya Fitch

Dedication

To all the versions of me, past and present
Thank you for surviving, healing, and remaining so full of love. Thank
you for finding your light. The world needs you.

Foreword

Sometime in my infancy I learned that love was a condition determined by the giver and that I was most often unlovable. In the pain of that loneliness I befriended art. Poetry became the place I could pour it all out when the grief threatened to consume me. It became the only way I knew how to sooth the ache. That is where this journey of healing and art began. As I aged and took the time to try dismantle the trauma of my youth through a degree in psychology, deep study of spirituality, and learning a variety of energy work modalities; I realized art was an ever present companion. I also learned love is something that I could cultivate within and that has no condition there in my own heart. I found healing when I learned how to step outside the pain and create the life I want. This book is a window into that journey. I wanted to share these works because I know there is someone out there that needs to know even in the midst of pain you can find peace. Even in your loneliness you can find love. It starts with the journey within. As you touch that pain and name it you give it a new place to live. Removed from your heart and living on the page it can open up space for hope and healing to enter. As I share these fragments of my pain, hope, and healing; it is my heart's greatest desire that you find a spark of resonance that delivers you to your own. I hope at the Crossroads of HeArtache and Healing you find your way home.

HeArtache

What Would Happen

What would happen if I wrote it all down?
Every word that passed over my heart
With the same ease and frequency of the breath flowing past my lips
What would happen if I let all the wounds show?
Like the tiny pores of my skin unseen but necessary to let the outside in
                                  yet a barrier keeping the outside from within
                hiding blemishes with dimples and the curved cheeks of a grin
What would happen then?
If through every unseen crack pain seeped
And every laugh pulled up covers to hide shoulders bent in love
                        because under the grief that's all there really was…
What would happen then?
If I showed you who I was?
What if I let you hear my art?
What if I let you see my heart?
What would happen then?

Echos in the chambers of a broken heart

There are ghosts here
Voices long faded
Smiles decaying
Haunted memories dancing to old love songs
Not realizing the loves gone
Yet they keep shuffling on
Echos heard only in the chambers of my broken heart

Sonya Fitch

Dams or Destruction

There are dams inside of me
Rivers held back by solid walls
Lakes formed to hold waters still enough to swim,
$\qquad\qquad\qquad\qquad$ but deep enough to drown
Glassy surfaces with gentle waves that crash against rocky shores,
$\qquad\qquad$ but should the dam break they would be no more
Can a damn hold back the ocean's reach as she calls forth my streams
$\qquad$ and rivers to rise and drain and complete the endless cycle
Is it love or pain
The water temperature feels the same
But the current will catch you and drag you beneath
Best to stay in the lakes
A safe place should the damn break

Suck it Up

One tear
Two tears
One sob
Two muffled cries
One sniffle
Two deep breaths
As I suck it all back inside
Can't have momentary meltdowns turning into unpredictable landslides
I might be buried alive by the pain inside

Sonya Fitch

Hiding

There's a sadness that lives inside me
She hides her tears behind smiles
Her broken-heart covered in brightly color clothes
Noone would know she's lives in the dark

Panic Attack

Seized
Icy fingers tighten grip
My heart arrested
Anxiety cloaked in black robes and chains
Pointed scythe turned wicked wand
Transforms open airways in swollen tubes
Choking on nothing but tongue
Vessels burst
Vision blurs
No place to go for blood or air
Sinking into despair
Cold arms catch me there
Lay me down to sleep
Death…
hazily I feel it take me
CLEAR!
Somewhere in the back of my ear I hear
Sweet air fill my lungs
I cough and sputter like I've swallowed water
Hand to chest
Heart beats again
Vision clearing
Head still blaring
Tears dried on tired cheeks
The mirror reveals the truth on my face
No defibrillator
A sense of will instead
It was never death
But fear who held me in a sense of dread
What a cruel game to play

Sonya Fitch

Fear has always been a fake
So good at changing faces
Adorned in illusion
Only the chains were real
If I could just remember
the weight
they feel
I might not be tricked again
back into panic's hands

One of those days

Some days are meant for sad songs, pillows, and fluffy things
When I need to pour out the overflow of my pain
Soft blankets soak up my tears
Teddy bears keep my secrets
They'll never tell what their glass eyes saw of my agony
My breaking
They'll smile just like me
And we'll play pretend
Everything is okay

Sonya Fitch

Abandoned

I am not the person who leaves people
I am the person people leave
I have only ever given up on love long after it has become a cold
                                        and empty hollowed space...
drafty with the remembrance of what was
Until I have emptied every ounce of love trying to fill the void
                        just to realize it has seeped through the cracks
                                        and I too am hollow
Left with a breeze that whispers of my longing
Until even the breath is gone
And so then am I
No, I am not the person who leaves
You left me long ago

Laughing through the Pain

Why is it that we turn our pain into a joke?
Laugh through tears and heartbreak that is so stuck in our throat we think
we'll choke?
Is it survival?
The will to breathe?
So we dislodge blocked airways with finding funny in the grief
Is it the silver lining on a heavy cloud that says I can still see the sky?
Is it because we still chase the gold at the bottom of fading rainbows
because we will not let hope die?
I think it's because laughter means we're still alive
That no matter the trauma we are going through somehow we survive
And that irony is hilarity
The world's greatest joke
Pain will not kill you,
But the inability to laugh at it will
Clear the lump in your throat
Breath through the tears
Find a way to see humor in your greatest fears
It will keep you here when you feel your grip slipping
Keep laughing
Until sunlight fades rainbows to blue skies
And grey clouds turn white
Laughter is a reminder you are still alive

Sonya Fitch

Her Eyes

And she could see through to your soul with her eyes
Yet she was blind to those who would take her heart with none to offer
And so she always gave freely of her love
but without any to refill
her heart became an empty offer
Yet she spent her whole life looking for a love that would be fulfilling
Now her eyes could see to your soul but they've lost their vision
Along with her smile,
they hide the pain so welll
For she loved but was never loved by another
And having given all of her love she was lost in hell
And her eyes could see the potential
And they could see light
But she was blind

Pain is Beauty

And I have laid my soul bare
Do you like what you see?
Is my pain pretty?
How about my tears?
Aren't the scars beautiful
As pretty as my tears…
You know… the ones that are wide open and I haven't stitched

together

yet…

Look here
Each mark in my existence is mapped out in them
Do you want to join me?
Share in my pain?
Oh just another wound to add…
Okay design away

Sonya Fitch

The Storm

There's a storm inside me
It's coming to a head
All the thoughts and emotions like a razor's edge
Ripping through my comfort
Tearing through my peace
The lack of love I feel inside, a hammer to my knees
There's a storm inside me
and I can feel its rage
Despite how hard I try to smile, lightning strikes again
And wind whips, and the rain falls, and I feel that I might shatter,
                        but I know there is a purpose to this natural disaster
It's cleansing me,
Making me new,
Even though its pain
I know when it is over…
The sun will shine again

Envy

Envy is a thief of joy
Always looking at someone else's plate
Never satisfied with her hand
She asks why can't I have that
Wished away her whole life
Missed joy getting stuck in the sad

Sonya Fitch

Willow

In her life there was pain
but there was also beauty
And though at times she bent with grief,
her feet stayed steady like the roots of a tree
And she would seek solace in the beauty,
and shake off the pain
She was like the Willow

Heart Break

I am not sure if I'll survive it,
The slow unraveling of my heart…
Each day another layer torn away,
Tear after tear I become undone
I try to smile
I try to love
I try to forgive
But this life, this world
is hurting me
And broken my heart is

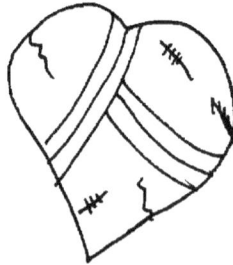

Sonya Fitch

Holding On

Isn't it funny how you fight to stay
As if there's something worth holding your soul in this place
Another day in the God forsaken rat race
We are not the same…
Or perhaps a better fit
Opposite ends of polarity
Instead of fighting to stay I'm fighting not to leave
Sounds almost the same until you look close enough to see
I'm barely holding on to this hellscape
Don't you feel it?
The days when your skin is too tight?
When to be inside your own body cuts like a million little knives?
Like you might die just from the sheer pain inside?
Oh no…
Just me?
Not surprisingly
Alone in a world full of people running the race but not a single one running to embrace
Love
Imagine being alone in love with no-one share it
I fight to stay here because it's torture to be
Loneliness calls me back to souls home
A place where love remembers me
I only stay because I'm told the journey is not yet done… still I am not quite sure why I'm holding on…

Lost

A leaf on the wind
Too early torn from the branch
Lost on borrowed time

Sonya Fitch

Shipwreck

Who's driving this ship
A question frequently asked but rarely answered
Why is the body likened to such a vessel anyway?
Is it because it rocks and sways with emotion?
Bracing for waves like it's afloat in the turbulent waters of the ocean?
Makes me think of the titanic
Who's failure was that?
Poor design or captains lack?
Back to the question of who is driving this?
Are we on our way to our own demise?
Soon to sink to Bottomless depths?
Wreckage never to be retrieved from it's watery death?
Someone better take the wheel before we are ship wrecked

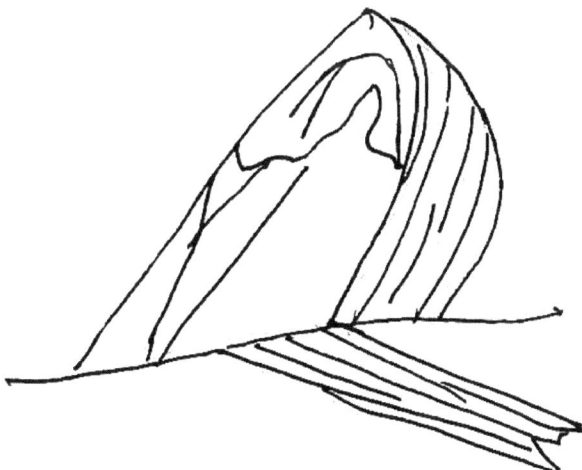

Shattered

I still haven't found all the pieces
Maybe they are gone forever
But I've desperately tried
over and over
To put myself back together
Bleeding fingers
Full of slivers and shards
Its the tiniest parts that are the most sharp
And I'm afraid of one more blow
I might not survive it
I am still missing pieces
Bleeding from the process
Of breaking
I'm more than fragile
I'm fragments of what I used to be
Strewn in patterns of loose resemblance
Like a crime scene
Or ancient artifacts dug out the dirt
Partially assembled fossiled bones that might soon turn to dust
One wrong move and I'll be back where I was
Shattered

Sonya Fitch

Who are you?

Who is this that's been hiding in the dark
Waiting for the sun to set
To bask in the dim light of the moon
Don't you know it still luminous
Your curves are on display
Sillouhette bent by the days pressure
Your tears glisten when starlight winks
Crickets play violin to the sound of your sobs
Your face is still grazed by the light
Bathing beauty on your plight
Like midnight flowers in bloom
You fight to hide but your light still stands austere
Against the shadows cast by the moon

Who is this who pretends to hide
Who cages the sun's rays inside
Prisms of colors caught like sharp pains in your rib cage
Who is this succumb to sorrow
Forgetting the nights alive
Watching while you grieve
Attending the wake of a life you cast aside
Who is this

And who might you be if you let the sun rise
If you watched dawn paint the sky
If you caught your reflection in morning dew
And stood face tilted to sun
Letting your tears dry in the warmth

If you let a smile grace your lips
Birds might pause their song to listen to your laughter
And butterflies might swoon at the sight of your beauty
You're a rare flower in the sun
Or so I remember
Don't you remember
Who you are

Sonya Fitch

Addict

Maybe I'll always crave it
And maybe I never knew
 what "it" really was
But the absence is so wide
It would take a lifetime
to fill the void
So I ache
Contemplating
Constantly
What would it take
Just to get a little taste
Of love

Weep

Even the trees weep
Resin seeping to seal
Resin seeping to heal
Sacred tears we gather and steep
Turning pain into something sweet
Syrup a balm for tongue
Yet it remembers the wounds it leaked from
Transformed into something new
What becomes of the tears that seep from you?

Sonya Fitch

The Battle

I still wage wars inside me
Pain versus peace
Healing versus traumatized
Loving versus enraged
Most days calm is winning and love is tending the wounds
But every so often sadness arranges a coup
Decimating the healing process with one fell swoop
The heart rallies what remains and fights to higher ground again
More healing
More loving
More cleansing tears
Then another attack
Except this time it's fear
Exposing weaknesses
Revealing hidden leaks
Infiltrators pretending to be a part of peace
Masked in false smiles with too much teeth
Innocence somehow still present yet to naïve to see
Somethings like the wolf in nursery rhymes
Dressed in sheep's clothing
Working from the inside
A devastating blow to ego and pride
But spirit won't let hope die
And so she raises her sword
Battle cry piercing through the thickest armor
Truth a poison on the tip
Wielding both death and medicine her tongue is both shield and defense

And she fights when all seems lost
Sometimes on her own
Single-handedly pushing pain into retreat,
But the battle is far from over
And the victory has yet to be claimed

Sonya Fitch

Lunar Eclipse

Lunar eclipse
Shadowed face
Darkening of already dark spaces
What do you hide in your shade?
What do you call forth to be released?
It's like playing a guessing game
Except who can win against the fates?
Karma follows my footsteps hidden in my own silhouette
I can't see her but I feel her presence
Foreboding like death
When she reaches for me what hand will she grab?
Right or left?
How have I lived?
Could it be she'll bestow a gift?
I won't know until it's light again
By then there will be nothing left to do but accept
That's the darkness of the lunar eclipse

Which Is it?

Some days I can't tell if happy is the illusion
If content is a daydream
When the pain surfaces I remember that it is all there has ever been
And I can't tell if I've buried it under delusion or it's truly dead
Is this a new pain
Or the same one that lives?
Clawing back up from the grave
Dirty fingers wrapped round my neck
Choking joy out until I can't catch my breath
Lights go dim
I can't see anything but the pain wrapped around me
Piercing through my heart
A familiar agony and I wonder how I've made it this far?
What do I do again?
to break free?
How can I bury this demon finally?
Do I need special chains ?
Spells and Incantations?
An exorcism…
A hug?
Oh yeah
You need love to be hugged
If that's what keeps the pain at bay
No wonder I so often feel this way
Who truly loves me?
Only me is what it seems
Maybe

Sonya Fitch

Sometimes on the good days
Apparently not enough
And I can't hug myself

I Almost Froze to Death

I almost froze to death
Caught in the cold
I stood still
Thought maybe if I held my ground
I could survive the onslaught
Hunkered down under blankets and prayed for luck
But to beat the cold you must keep moving
Freezing will end up with you frozen
You have to keep going
I started to notice my breath was slowing
Frost bitten lips
I knew if I stayed longer my heart might be next
I could almost feel it freezing in my chest
So I dragged myself up and out of my quest
First a brisk walk
Then I ran
Towards the shelter of my sanctity
You were the arctic
But I could see the northern lights
And I decided the sky is much to beautiful to lay down and die
I took back my life
But I still remember that time
I almost froze to death

Sonya Fitch

The Burden

I carried it
All these years on my back
The weight of every mistake I ever made
Never good enough for anything
Stained
Thought I was cursed at birth
So I broadened my shoulders to carry the load
My karmic debt that I was sure I was bestowed
It could not possibly be the way I raised
Or the things that I seen
Or the people allowed into my home
Or the home I never really had
Or the eight schools
Or the countless left behind pets
Lost diaries
Teddy bears
And bibles
Frowned on by God
The betraying disciple
Fornicator
Fast
Floozy
That is putting it politely
Also
Fat
Failure
Snake
There's more but there are only so many pages
Pages of my life when I wondered why I was born

What was the point if all I could do was wrong
If I was so unlovable
Even by God
Repentance
Marriage to the father of my children
Born out of wedlock
Teen mom
I thought maybe that would fix it in the eyes of God
But I didn't believe
So maybe I'd just go to hell
Perhaps I'd been living in purgatory all along
My punishment for every failure and wrong
A car accident consequence and warning for all my sins
I tried to live saintly
Be a good wife
Mother
Cheated on
It was my fault I couldn't be everything he wanted
I wasn't enough
But I still left
Couldn't bear the pain
Just to wind up with more of the same
Except now I was a terrible mother
Exposing my children to a different type of monster
It was my fault
I should have known
I knew I was cursed
That's why even my pets couldn't survive
Took a risk to bring new furry friends in and they died
Must be payment for keeping my children alive
These were the thoughts that swam in my head

Sonya Fitch

I was so poisonous
Men just quit their jobs to live off of me
And develop a deep hatred or void filled with ice
Broken hearts were the price of being in my life
It was my fault
I was born this way
Then I remembered the innocence they say every baby is born with
What happened to me?
It could not possibly be the way I was raised
Or the things that I seen
Or the people allowed into my home
Or the home I never really had
Or the eight schools
Or the countless left behind pets
Lost diaries
Teddy bears
And bibles
Frowned on by God
Cursed before I even took a breath
I carried it
Everyday
The weight of every mistake
The Guilt and the Shame
Until today
When I realized
It's not even sane
To measure my worth by a life shaped for me
It was never my fault
Not even in my hands
But the rest of my life is

So I put down the bags
Stood up straight
hands free for the first time
To create my life by my own design
I picked up the pen
And started to write

Sonya Fitch

Handle With Care

I don't have a lot of baggage but I do have a lot of scars
The kind that ache when the weather changes or you hit it just right
I don't carry the burden but my body still remembers
           in ever too tight seams of the wound that once ripped it bare
Be careful how you touch me please
When you graze those scars the pain flares
Hard to know when they're invisible I'm sure
So just handle me with care
Treat me like a sacred thing and there's no reason to fear
But forget my fragility and be prepared
If you cannot be trusted to be gentle
I may not let you near

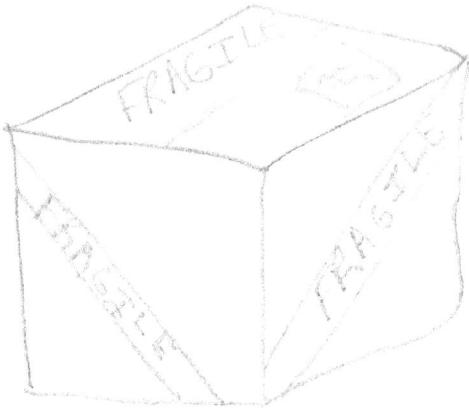

Afraid of Heights

I've had to let go so many times
It's no wonder why I don't reach for more
Why grasp for something I can never hold?
If it was never truly mine, why try to hold on just to let go?
How do you aspire to reach for the stars
when through parted fingers it does fall?
Or to embrace love, warm and sweet
To find yourself cradling shoulders of your own?
Gracefully, I say
All things flow
Nothing is mine
It's okay to let go
But still I do not know then how to believe what I want
will surely be mine,
When I know just as surely it will leave?
Better not to want
Better not to reach
Less is the brokenheart for the love it never intends to keep
Stories I tell myself to protect my inner peace?
Or stories I tell myself to keep my heart in chains?
The answers to these questions remain yet to be seen

Sonya Fitch

Ice Bath

Pain pools around me
A familiar bath of ice
Deep breathing
I plunge in
Cold threatens to steal my air
But I've trained for this
I know how to find the rhythm
Slowly
In and Out
Not so bad now
Almost finished
You can survive the cold if you just control your breath
Pain passes
I'm in the warmth again

Sonya Fitch

The Crossroads

The poems you just read came from some of the darkest places inside of me, or perhaps it would be better to say some of the darkest times in my life. It is easy to equate darkness to pain and sorrow just as I have here, however, I have also found that in my darkness I gained my voice. My greatest source of creativity was born from these deep places of pain. There I witnessed the pieces of myself that needed to be seen and heard. These shadowed pieces of my pain were the shields I carried in attempts to protect my heart. Some of these poems are expression of my sadness. Others are of anger and defeat. All of them are faces of shadows that I walked in for a period of time in my life. Even now the right wound might bring a shadow to my face, but by naming the shadows I was able to put them in a place outside of my heart and bring them into the light. By giving voice to the pain it no longer festered in my body. More so, it showed me I how I felt in an abstract way that I could better understand. Now when I recognize the shields coming up and swords coming out I know what it means and I can choose a different way. One that is rooted in love. This is what art has been for me. A place to take the pieces of my soul and puts them into the world to give them life in a way that doesn't overshadow the light I'm intended to shine. By illuminating these parts of myself and their purpose I was able to work towards healing. It is my goal to give you some insight on how you might be able to do the same thing for yourself. To do so I would like to tell you more about the process I used to create the crossroads between heartache and healing. Shadow work.

As I alluded, the shadow is a part or parts of the self that reside in darkness. Not necessarily bad, but frequently not identified or acknowledged because it is rooted in some form of pain, fear, or shame. Shadows are the personalities and characteristics we develop to hide the pieces of ourselves we don't want to see, share, and/or feel. We all have them. They form, as we progress through life, from emotional wounds, traumas, and otherwise difficult experiences that impact how we interact going forward. They are the unconscious habits and responses we form as a result. So while the shadow is our hidden truths, it can also be very visible in our day to day life through our actions. It's simply that we don't recognize it. Peter pan is a great example. Imagining your shadow running away from you? Well these shadows are kind of like that with one big exception. Instead of running away they are actually running the show without you even realizing. The process of cultivating a conscious awareness and working towards revealing and healing these shadowed aspects of self is called shadow work. By looking at these parts of ourselves to discover how and why they have developed we can begin to integrate them in a healthier way. Shadow work is the practice of intentionally looking deeper at some of our darker thoughts, habits, responses, and wounds to discover not only how they influence our lives, but how we can heal that aspect of ourselves. It teaches us to look at our emotions and recognize where they stem from. This recognition allows us to notice when the shadow rises and make a choice before we act. Through awareness the shadow cast over our perception and actions is lifted, giving us the lens of truth. The truth behind your actions and reactions, and the truth of who you are beyond and outside of them. With that truth you have the ability to reshape your world. It takes hard work, honesty, and time, but let me assure you it is some of the most rewarding work you can do. In this type of work you learn to identify yourself beyond the masks and truly listen to what your soul needs. Helping you to make healthier choices for your mind, body, spirit, and feel more emotionally balanced, confident, and secure. Shadow work teaches us to acknowledge and love every part of ourselves. Even the dark parts, because in that dark lays the seeds for growth.

Shadows are teachers much like our emotions. Perhaps because they are born of them. Formed through trials experienced during life, shadows are most often revealed during a trauma response. In that moment the shadow appears giving voice to the old wounds we still carry. Often though, the every day shadow lives with us as defense mechanism we have forgotten to disengage.

Sonya Fitch

They are a part of our everyday thoughts and interactions. They very well can be the ones in the driver seat stealing the enriched experience we could be having if we were only able to shed light on their need. See, the shadow forms to protect us from pain. They may choose anger, deflection, avoidance, pleasure, etc. No matter the choice of method, the shadow's goal is to never feel that same pain again.

So what does the everyday shadow look like?

Low self-esteem

Fear

Over-indulgence be it a substance or activity (sex, alcohol, people pleasing)

An inability to say no

Always feeling and saying sorry

Dominance

Indecisiveness and/or procrastination

Avoidance

Masking (hiding your true feelings or personality)

These are just some of the shadows that can be present but unseen on a regular basis. These shadows hide in plain sight and steal our opportunity to be fully present in our lives. My approach to integration is to reassign or reimagine the role the shadow is trying to fulfill. That is why awareness is important. Looking at the underlying emotion we can begin to sort out the reasons and think about how we might better honor our boundaries and safety with new tools.

These common defense mechanisms are your fight, flight, freeze and fawn responses.

These are the primal defenses that everyone naturally has. Intended to be situational, this primal defense system, when left engaged is how, the shadow develops. Triggered in the moment we feel threatened by anything that resembles the original wound, our shadows act as a shield to prevent further trauma. Be it continued presence in unsafe spaces or the high stress of today's world, the issues arise when we never lower the shield. You cannot see fully what is in front of you and you cannot fully be seen. It draws a veil over perception and truth.

So the question is, have you noticed your own shadow? If these poems have echoed with resonance in your heart its likely you are already at the crossroads of heartache and ready to start down the road towards healing. Here are some writing prompts you can explore to help in your journey.

Reflect-
What emotional reactions have you noticed that come up during stressful or triggering moments?

What experiences bring up these type of reactions?

Do you remember the first time you felt that way?

Can you relate the emotions you uncovered to past experiences or wounds?

Recognize-
Can you recognize a situation in your life that keeps repeating, perhaps in relationships, work, or self-care?

Think about how those might relate to the emotions you described above and make note of any patterns...
What would you like to change or keep?

Explore the masks you wear to manage these situations or emotions. Can you recognize any primal defenses?

Redefine-
Can you give these aspects of yourself names? Roles? What fears are they attempting to protect you from?

How can you integrate that in a healthier way such as boundaries or clear communication?

Thinking of what you learned create a dialogue with the shadows you've named.
Ask things like where did they come from?

What do they want? How can you help them be seen? How can you work together?

Integrate-
Consider safety; how might you create that feeling in healthy ways?

How about love? What ways can you be loving to yourself?

Where might you need boundaries and what do healthy boundaries look like?

Create constructive goals and checks for them to stay on track.

Perhaps the poems that strike a resonant string most within you will provide you a place to start. A name, a scale, or a witness… it is my hope that these glimpses of my wounds and salves I found to soothe them open a path for you to enter into your own shadowed spaces and light a candle. And another. And another. Until you've found yourself back in the bright light of your true essence. This is my offering: A candle in the dark to help you find your way.

Sonya Fitch

Healing

Healing

They say healing is like peeling the layers of an onion.
And sure, we cry with burning eyes as we make our way to the center,
	but I have another analogy for you.
What if healing is more like blooming?
Each petal unfolds to reveal the full beauty of the flower.

What if tears form as the petals fall and fade
	just for a new bloom to rise and take it's place?
See, I think healing is a lot like grief,
	and think grief is a by product of death
	but also love.

And if we weep in loss, shouldn't we also weep in joy
	because for every love celebrated for its time
	and mourned in death, there is a new life born
	love blooms again…. and again
For every version of you that you shed
	are you not becoming more and more beautiful in your essence --
A bud becoming the bloom?

Healing is the alchemy of living
and becoming is simply the transformation
	from seed to flower,
		again and again and again.
And there will be seasons…

Just remember after winter comes spring.

Vulnerability

What does vulnerability mean to me?
As I sit naked looking beneath
The masks of joy and the fear of rejection
The mask of healing and haunted house of pain
Protection?
All these faces I wear that cover who is under there
The real
Me in the rawest form
The me who is free
What does vulnerability mean?
It means somehow I've let you see
That your words can touch the tender soul
Who bruises easily and is fragile love
Love in all her many shades
Longing or embraced
She aches for and fears them both
That's the truth hidden under the clothes
What does vulnerability mean to me?
Naked and seen
Prepared for anything
Secure in self
Yet wondering
What will you do with me
Will your fingerprints leave a stain that I'll have to scrub clean
Healing
the soap that restores my soul
Burns on fresh wounds
Can I handle it?

Sonya Fitch

I suppose

Vulnerable because I let you in a place that requires softness
and gentle steps

And while I trust myself it's hard to trust other humans
I stare at the masks, the clothes, and the shields
Left to lay in a heap
Released
I look back in the mirror
To see the fragility of my radiance freed
Bareness is brave
This is vulnerability
See me

Flower-like Life

Nectar drips
Butterflies sip
Bumblebees dip

Does the flower wait on the insect?
No
She just blooms
Does the flower wait for the perfect match?
No
She gives of herself freely so her seeds are sown

Nature is whole and in harmony
It fulfills itself
Let your nectar drip
And nature will do the rest

Sonya Fitch

Love me

I'm writing a love letter to myself…
No, A love song
And endless melody of sweet everything because sweet nothings
no longer live in my heart
A song of joy and beauty and desire that never fades
A song that rises yet never peaks because there is no crescendo,
no ease or release
No this song rises in love like I rise through life
A love everlasting and it only ends when I take my last breath,
when this body dies

This is my love song
An ode to me
And the divine sacred goddess that I am

I love me for all time, with out limit or condition,
without fear or restraint. I love myself wholly
as a mother, daughter, sister, lover, as the way and the path
of my ancestors. I love myself like the sky at night
and the sunrise come each morning. Like the sun on my skin,
the rain on my windowsill, the breeze in trees,

or a frosty morning when all rests at peace.
I love myself universally and in this love I do not forget.
Not one note out of key, my voice cries out beautifully.
I love myself wholly.

I am holy
In this love I am free

Sonya Fitch

Black Butterfly

With wings like night
She took flight
From the depths of pain unknown
Each wound added to her grace
It was from the grief that she had grown
And as she flitted through moonlight
She was a beautiful and glorious sight
Made of magic and ready for life
A Mystical Black Butterfly

About Me

I could tell you about my broken heart
How it was shattered beyond recognition
The way I pieced it back together with millions of tiny stitches
But I'd rather tell you about my love
How it floods
and needs no vessel
My heart has been confused as the source
But love is my essence (and entire being)
Of course it'd be too much to store in such a fragile thing
It cannot be contained
So I let my love roam free
You can hear it when I speak
Feel it in my touch
See it in my steps
In my children's faces
Or the words I leave on pages
It's in my breath
More than the heartbeat in my chest
My love is existence
It is meant to be free
So I share it unabashedly
In a passing smile
A kind word
A hug
A picture of flowers with tiny bugs
Can't you tell love is all around
Not just meant for romance

Sonya Fitch

Love is a life dance
It's meant to spiral and prance
And play and touch everything
Because love is everything
And so am I
And so are we
And so are you

She is

She is pillows and valley
Soft and warm
Safe space to rest
Sacred place to recharge
She is contemplation
The tip of the tongue
Sage and Scribe
Sparked thought, wonder, and conversation
She is sex
Raw and rough
Gentle and sweet
Climax and creation
She is wrath
Sharp words
And sharper teeth
Daggered fingers
Warrior Queen
She is Woman
Temptress
Mother
Fighter
Friend
She
Is
Everything

Sonya Fitch

The Point

The point isn't to find someone to love
The point is to be loving.
The point isn't to always be happy
The point is to just be

Whole

I find myself in constant motion
Seeking, learning, growing
Not just for my betterment
But to become whole
What could be better than that feeling?
To know that I am me, and me is we, and we are one,
                                    and one is all of the infinite and eternity?
What could be better than feeling...that beat, a pulse not just in my heart,
                                            but in my soul?
I've caught glimpses, had tingles, held the world's hand for a moment
                                                    from time to time
I know the thrill and sheer beauty of that grand connection to all
And so I keep seeking, learning, growing
Not just for my betterment
But to become whole and live in the Divinity that is all things
            and nothing, but everything that is bigger than me yet still me
Where I am whole always and I never forget

Sonya Fitch

Morning

I like to rise slow
I am not quick to seize the hour
Opening curtains
I smile at sunshine
I have plans to ponder
First coffee
Then cards
Then a meditation &
Mood music
A poem to get the heart moving
Sunday mornings are lazy times for play
A cat demands her rubs
It's time to start the day

Gratitude

Light peaks through the window
Eyes mist for joy
Another morning comes
Sunrise painting the sky
And I am so blessed

A child calls her mother
She just wants to say hello
I love you
Grown but still reaching for my hand
And I am so blessed

Furballs curl around my feet
Purs vibrate healing from arched backs
Barks erupt from frantic wiggles just to flop for belly rubs
Animals express the most unconditional love
And I am so blessed

Floors creak like old bones
Paint flakes with layered memories of laughter and first loves
Faded scribbles evidence of what was
Sturdy still the roof that held the old and
now keeps the new
And I am so blessed

Sonya Fitch

Fertile fields full of life
Wildflowers, bumblebees, and dragonflies
Wrinkled like skin with memories of gardens
Soft carpet for barefeet
And I am so blessed

Moon peaking behind the pines
A million stars twinkle to life
Fireflys blink like a beacon of hope
Bright light for short lives
Kissed foreheads, and tight hugs
I say goodnight
And I am so blessed

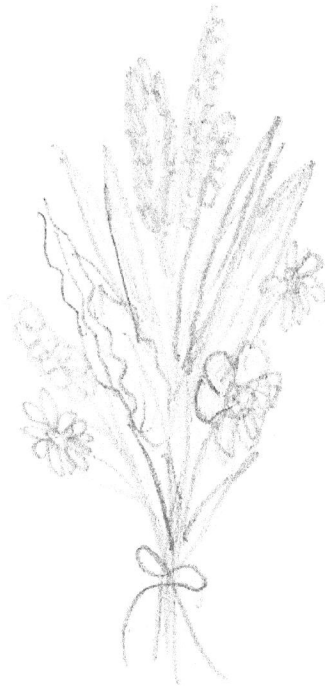

Fired Earth

The Virgin maid plants her wheat
Waiting for hooven feet
Enamored by the warmth of his flame
The archer blazes in to lay his claim

An unlikely pair and paradox
The sun and moon
Dancing together
They each concede a piece of their light
It would seem for one to live
the other must die
Instead they give each other life

Scorched earth in his wake
The centaur plants more than he takes
Seeds of the mind
Philosophizing life and spirituality
He shows her how to be free
She keeps him grounded to gather and share harvest
She taught him to plant his dreams

An unlikely pair and paradox
Night and Day
Polarities
On the lines of opposition someplace they meet
Sprouts breaking through singed soils
They learned to let each other breath
Fired Earth evidence of their unity

Sonya Fitch

Befriending Fear

I saw a scary sight today
Fear leapt up to shake her fists
She said to me,
Look at you in all your peace! What will you do with this?
Will you quake and quiver?
Will you act like you are blind?
Will you cry in pity?
What will it be this time?
I must admit it
There was a shock
That I shed some tears
I had to evaluate where they came from…
Were they mine? Or Fears?
I realized they were empathy
That I had the tools
That I didn't shake and shiver
But went straight into the action of do
I saw a scary sight today
But I didn't back away
I met her with a hug and said,
"Compassion is my way"

My Valentine

I have always hated this day
As long as I can remember
Watching love stroll by to be bestowed upon another
To be forgotten and overlooked or gifted with sympathy
I don't remember ever a time when love chose me
And so I chose myself
I started celebrating my own heart
Maybe I'm the only one who recognizes my worth
I always felt unlovable
But today I say
I am more than deserving
I still hate Valentine's Day
But I sure do love me

Sonya Fitch

Knots

I tied myself in knots for you
Just like I've pulled back unruly curls
Wrapped tight by a rubber band in a ponytail or bun
I twisted myself into a shape more pleasing to your taste
And just like that rubber band
I got stuck
Bands of conformance wrapped tight around will
Despite how I struggled against it
They kept holding me still

Scissors and ripped strands
I cut the rubber band free from my carefully combed tresses
Sword tongue and hard truths
I cut free of all the expectations
Ran my fingers through my new found freedom
Hair and Spirit wild
I remembered this is what I was born to be
God given greatness coursing through every fiber of my being
I started being
Exactly who I was
Before I got myself all twisted up
In Knots

Navigating Life

Why do we forget when it aches
That a moment ago there was no pain?
Why do we fail to remember in times of joy
There will be lows around the corner?
All these years and still can't see
Life is constantly changing
Shifting back and forth
It's up to you to stay on course
No matter what the seas of life bring
Calm waters
Or treacherous waves
Hold the wheel and stay steady
The stars still guide the way
And rainbows still break through clouds when the sun comes out again

Sonya Fitch

Releasing the Breath

I didn't know
How long it was held
How painfully close
I was to slipping from this world
How my vision had blurred
My thoughts had slowed
Fading to black
Until something said let go
And I released the breath

Life is a Gamble

Every time I get ready to fold
You deal another card
Perks me up to try one more time in this game of life
And just when I think that I'm all in
The odds are not in my favor
Somehow the spin
Keeps me alive again
You've taught me not waver
And so when fear comes and stands across the table
I put on my poker face and smile
It's not just luck that holds my hand
The universe is on my side
Oh, look
Jackpot
I win

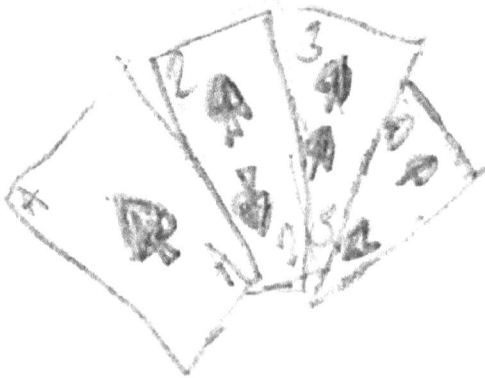

Sonya Fitch

Art's Entrance

Do you ever wonder where people find their art?
Is it a place of love that forms the spark?
Or like me,
did it begin with pain?
See… I found my voice under broken things
Sifting through shattered pieces of my heart
Sorting through the jagged edges of destroyed dreams
I stumbled upon the words to identify the catastrophe that was me

Me

A house made from glass that had met a stone
And thought it was beautiful until it was thrown
And then marveled at the wreckage of the shards small and large
                                    that lay where once walls were
And to this day I can't decide if the container was meant
                                    to keep me inside or the others out
but it doesn't matter now because I was torn down… to the foundation
And there etched in stone was the cure
The explicit directions to pick myself up
Sweep aside what crumbled and start again
Recycle what you can and throw out the trash
There in the rubble I found my art
Piece by piece I rebuilt my heart
Strung back together my dreams
Used blood and tears as paint, to create stained glass murals
                    of what used to be and then reinforced them with love

Permanent reminders of what was and beautifully illustrated boundaries
Hidden doors with locks and keys

Reserved for the deserving
When you walk by you see a masterpiece

Yes, me

Built on the foundation that couldn't be broken
Standing on words that longed to be spoken
Turning wreckage into love
Using hope as the design
promise as the furniture
words to illustrate the walls
Things like
Worthy
Beautiful
Strong
And Sacred
I designated a room to prayer and patience
Built my own safe spaces
Made myself into a mansion
Not like those cold marble places
No, I'm bright colors and warm intimate placements
Everywhere I turn there's another facet
Fabric woven like a tapestry
I am a patchwork of everything I've experienced
                                        reinterpreted into a gallery
To know me is to witness living art
Pain may have been the start but love is where I begin again
                                and again   and again

Sonya Fitch

Love Like Poetry

I want a love that feels like poetry
No, Not the kind that bleeds
The kind that breaths

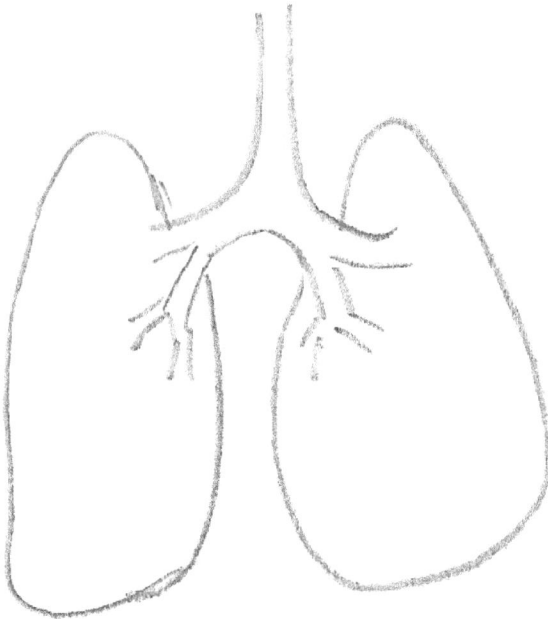

Remodeling

Old doors creak with whispers of what was
Will new paint bring back some life
I think as Flakes trail in dust
Perhaps the wood should be stripped bare
Hardware replaced

Old doors lead to nowhere
That's my fear
But refinished
Maybe they lead to my prayers
Knob turns
I guess I have to start somewhere

Sonya Fitch

Remove the Mask

Anger is just a mask for sadness
Sadness is just a mask for longing
Longing is just another face of love
Take the masks off

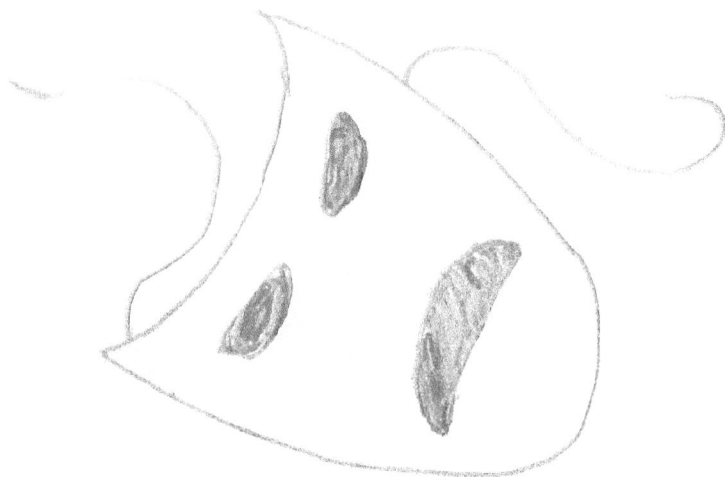

Emotional Blockage

Emotional Blockage
Fear is nothing more than bottled waters
Remove the cork and let them flow

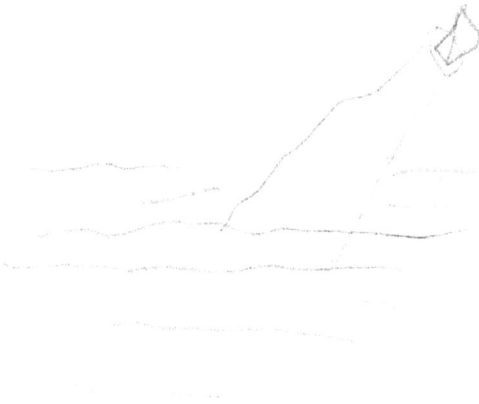

Sonya Fitch

The Difference

Hope and fear often wear the same clothing
But they fit different
Fear's outfits are tight in all the wrong places
While Hope's are comfortable and compliment your figure
Pay attention to how you feel in your clothes

Metamorphosis

Dissolving in darkness
Melting into a malleable mold
Holding hands with Death
Transformed from the old
There is no permanence
Why do they grieve
Unfolding fresh wings
I am made new

Sonya Fitch

Keep Going

Not all seeds grow
Some sprout just to die
But gardeners don't cling to the skeleton of what was
They nurture what remains and prepare the soil for the next seedling

Planted

Under layers of dark
Seeds begin to sprout
And roots start to form
Preparing for the returning sun
Stretching out
The work has begun
Soon to bloom
With fruit abundant

Sonya Fitch

Will-O-Wisp

I glanced a tiny flame
Watched her dance and wave
She reminded me that is where it all starts
Just one small flame brings light to the dark
Illuminating whats unseen
Just one flicker sparks light to life
Perhaps these little spirits are named for their strength
It only takes a wisp of will to chase your dreams
Even on the darkest day
Follow the light they say
I say follow the flame

colophon
Wider Perspectives Publishing artists published – the list reworked due to the growing library of fine writers coming out of, or even into, the Hampton Roads area of Virginia.

Samantha Casey
Donna Burnett-Robinson
Faith Griffin
Se'Mon-Michelle Rosser
Lisa M. Kendrick
Cassandra IsFree
Nich (Nicholis Williams)
Samantha Geovjian Clarke
Natalie Morison-Uzzle
Gus Woodward II
Patsy Bickerstaff
Edith Blake
Jack Cassada
Dezz
Daniel Garwood
Jada Hollingsworth
Tabetha Moon House
Travis Hailes- Virgo, thePoet
Nick Marickovich
Grey Hues
Rivers Raye
Madeline Garcia
Chichi Iwuorie
Symay Rhodes
Tanya Cunningham
(Scientific Eve)
Terra Leigh
Raymond M. Simmons
Samantha Borders-Shoemaker
Taz Weysweete'
Ann Shalaski

Jade Leonard
Serena Fusek
Darean Polk
Bobby K. (The Poor Man's Poet)
J. Scott Wilson (Teech!)
Charles Wilson
Gloria Darlene Mann
Neil Spirtas
Jorge Mendez & JT Williams
Sarah Eileen Williams
Stephanie Diana (Noftz)
Shanya – Lady S.
Jason Brown (Drk Mtr)
Kailyn Rae Sasso
Crickyt J. Expression
Luana Portales

Crystal Nolen
Catherine TL Hodges
Kent Knowlton
Maria April C.
James Harry Wilson
Bruce Curb
Willy J. (Jason Williams)

the Hampton Roads Artistic Collective (757 Perspectives) & The Poet's Domain are all WPP literary journals in cooperation with Scientific Eve or Live Wire Press

Check for those artists on FaceBook, Instagram, the Virginia Poetry Online channel on YouTube, and other social media.

Sonya Fitch

www.ingramcontent.com/pod-product-compliance
Lightning Source LLC
Chambersburg PA
CBHW071354090426
42738CB00012B/3118